Great Women in History

Clara Barton

by Erin Edison

Consulting Editor: Gail Saunders-Smith, PhD

Consultant: Dr. Brie Swenson Arnold
Assistant Professor of History
Coe College, Cedar Rapids, Iowa

CAPSTONE PRESS
a capstone imprint

Pebble Books are published by Capstone Press,
1710 Roe Crest Drive, North Mankato, Minnesota 56003.
www.capstonepub.com

Library of Congress Cataloging-in-Publication Data
Edison, Erin.
  Clara Barton / by Erin Edison.
      p. cm.—(Pebble books. Great women in history)
  Includes bibliographical references and index.
  ISBN 978-1-62065-076-9 (library binding)
  ISBN 978-1-62065-857-4 (paperback)
  ISBN 978-1-4765-1626-4 (eBook PDF)
  1. Barton, Clara, 1821-1912—Juvenile literature. 2. Nurses—United States—
Biography—Juvenile literature. 3. American Red Cross—Biography—Juvenile
literature. I. Title.
  HV569.B3E35 2013
  361.7′634092—dc23
  [B]   2012033472

Note to Parents and Teachers

The Great Women in History set supports national social studies
standards related to people and culture. This book describes and
illustrates Clara Barton. The images support early readers in
understanding the text. The repetition of words and phrases helps
early readers learn new words. This book also introduces early
readers to subject-specific vocabulary words, which are defined
in the Glossary section. Early readers may need assistance to read
some words and to use the Table of Contents, Glossary, Read More,
Internet Sites, and Index sections of the book.

Printed in the United States of America in Stevens Point, Wisconsin.
092012   006937WZS13

Table of Contents

1821

born

Early Life

Civil War nurse Clara Barton
was born December 25, 1821,
in Massachusetts. Her parents were
Stephen and Sarah Barton.
Clara had two older brothers
and two older sisters.

◀ Clara's birthplace in North Oxford, Massachusetts

1821
born

1833
cares for
injured brother

Clara's brothers and sisters taught her reading and math.

In 1833 Clara's brother David was hurt in a fall. Clara cared for her brother for two years until he was better.

David Barton during the Civil War

1821
born

1833
cares for
injured brother

1839
becomes
a teacher

8

Young Adult

In 1839 Clara took and passed

a test to become a teacher.

At this time, teaching was

one of the only jobs for women.

Clara enjoyed teaching.

She treated her students

with fairness and respect.

1821 born

1833 cares for injured brother

1839 becomes a teacher

1852 starts a public school

In 1852 Clara started Bordentown,

New Jersey's first public school.

But because she was a woman,

Clara was not allowed to be

in charge of the school.

She left the school in 1854.

 Clara's school in Bordentown

1821
born

1833
cares for
injured brother

1839
becomes
a teacher

1852
starts a
public school

Clara moved to Washington, D.C.,
to work in the U.S. Patent Office.
By April 1861, the Civil War
had begun. Clara wanted to serve
her country. She was among the first
to collect supplies for soldiers.

1861

Civil War
begins

1821
born

1833
cares for
injured brother

1839
becomes
a teacher

1852
starts a
public school

14

Life's Work

Clara brought food, clothing, and medical supplies to soldiers. She cared for wounded men during dangerous battles. Soldiers called Clara the "Angel of the Battlefield." It was during the Civil War that women first became nurses.

1861
Civil War begins

1821
born

1833
cares for
injured brother

1839
becomes
a teacher

1852
starts a
public school

At the end of the war, President Abraham Lincoln asked Clara to find missing soldiers. Clara sent soldiers' names to post offices and newspapers. People sent information to Clara. By 1869 she had helped find 22,000 missing or dead soldiers.

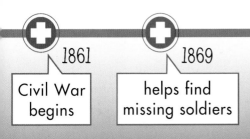

1861
Civil War
begins

1869
helps find
missing soldiers

1821
born

1833
cares for
injured brother

1839
becomes
a teacher

1852
starts a
public school

In 1881 Clara formed

the American Red Cross.

This group gives food, medicine,

and other supplies to people hurt

by wars or disasters.

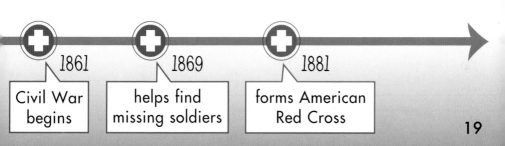

1861
Civil War
begins

1869
helps find
missing soldiers

1881
forms American
Red Cross

1821
born

1833
cares for
injured brother

1839
becomes
a teacher

1852
starts a
public school

Later Life

Clara led the Red Cross for more than 20 years. In 1912 Clara died at age 90. But the work she started with the American Red Cross continues today.

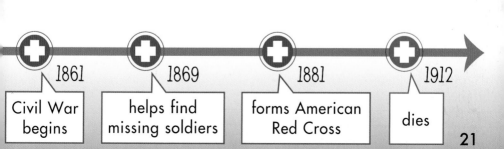

1861
Civil War begins

1869
helps find missing soldiers

1881
forms American Red Cross

1912
dies

Glossary

Civil War—the U.S. war fought between the northern states and the southern states over slavery; the Civil War lasted from 1861 to 1865

disaster—an event that causes great damage, loss, or suffering

respect—the belief in the quality and worth of others and yourself

wound—an injury or cut

Read More

Dubowski, Cathy East. *Clara Barton: I Want to Help!* Defining Moments. New York: Bearport Pub. Co., 2006.

Dunn, Joeming. *Clara Barton.* Edina, Minn.: Magic Wagon, 2009.

Wade, Mary Dodson. *Amazing Civil War Nurse Clara Barton.* Amazing Americans. Berkeley Heights, N.J.: Enslow Publishers, 2010.

Internet Sites

FactHound offers a safe, fun way to find Internet sites related to this book. All of the sites on FactHound have been researched by our staff.

Here's all you do:

Visit *www.facthound.com*

Type in this code: 9781620650769

Super-cool stuff! Check out projects, games and lots more at
www.capstonekids.com

Index

Word Count: 291
Grade: 1
Early-Intervention Level: 24

Editorial Credits
Erika L. Shores, editor; Alison Thiele, designer; Wanda Winch, media researcher; Jennifer Walker, production specialist